ISBN 978-1-333-78164-4
PIBN 10544920

This book is a reproduction of an important historical work. Forgotten Books uses
state-of-the-art technology to digitally reconstruct the work, preserving the original format
whilst repairing imperfections present in the aged copy. In rare cases, an imperfection in
the original, such as a blemish or missing page, may be replicated in our edition. We do,
however, repair the vast majority of imperfections successfully; any imperfections that
remain are intentionally left to preserve the state of such historical works.

1 MONTH OF
FREE
READING

at

www.ForgottenBooks.com

By purchasing this book you are eligible for one month membership to ForgottenBooks.com, giving you unlimited access to our entire collection of over 700,000 titles via our web site and mobile apps.

To claim your free month visit:

www.forgottenbooks.com/free544920

English
Français
Deutsche
Italiano
Español
Português

www.forgottenbooks.com

Mythology Photography **Fiction**
Fishing Christianity **Art** Cooking
Essays Buddhism Freemasonry
Medicine **Biology** Music **Ancient**
Egypt Evolution Carpentry Physics
Dance Geology **Mathematics** Fitness
Shakespeare **Folklore** Yoga Marketing
Confidence Immortality Biographies
Poetry **Psychology** Witchcraft
Electronics Chemistry History **Law**
Accounting **Philosophy** Anthropology
Alchemy Drama Quantum Mechanics
Atheism Sexual Health **Ancient History**
Entrepreneurship Languages Sport
Paleontology Needlework Islam
Metaphysics Investment Archaeology
Parenting Statistics Criminology
Motivational

0^4

COPYRIGHT ACT TECHNICAL CORRECTIONS

Y 4. J 89/1:104/32

Copyright Act Technical Corrections...

HEARING

BEFORE THE

SUBCOMMITTEE ON
COURTS AND INTELLECTUAL PROPERTY

OF THE

COMMITTEE ON THE JUDICIARY
HOUSE OF REPRESENTATIVES

ONE HUNDRED FOURTH CONGRESS

FIRST SESSION

ON

H.R. 1861

TO MAKE TECHNICAL CORRECTIONS IN THE SATELLITE HOME VIEWER ACT OF 1994 AND OTHER PROVISIONS OF TITLE 17, UNITED STATES CODE

NOVEMBER 9, 1995

Serial No. 32

Printed for the use of the Committee on the Judiciary

U.S. GOVERNMENT PRINTING OFFICE

22–160 CC   WASHINGTON : 1996

For sale by the U.S. Government Printing Office
Superintendent of Documents, Congressional Sales Office, Washington, DC 20402
ISBN 0-16-052350-8

COPYRIGHT ACT TECHNICAL CORRECTIONS

04

Y 4. J 89/1: 104/32

Copyright Act Technical Corrections...

ᴴᴱᴬᴿING

BEFORE THE

SUBCOMMITTEE ON
COURTS AND INTELLECTUAL PROPERTY

OF THE

COMMITTEE ON THE JUDICIARY
HOUSE OF REPRESENTATIVES

ONE HUNDRED FOURTH CONGRESS

FIRST SESSION

ON

H.R. 1861

TO MAKE TECHNICAL CORRECTIONS IN THE SATELLITE HOME
VIEWER ACT OF 1994 AND OTHER PROVISIONS OF TITLE 17,
UNITED STATES CODE

NOVEMBER 9, 1995

Serial No. 32

Printed for the use of the Committee on the Judiciary

U.S. GOVERNMENT PRINTING OFFICE

22–160 CC   WASHINGTON : 1996

For sale by the U.S. Government Printing Office
Superintendent of Documents, Congressional Sales Office, Washington, DC 20402
ISBN 0-16-052350-8

COMMITTEE ON THE JUDICIARY

HENRY J. HYDE, Illinois, *Chairman*

CARLOS J. MOORHEAD, California
F. JAMES SENSENBRENNER, JR., Wisconsin
BILL McCOLLUM, Florida
GEORGE W. GEKAS, Pennsylvania
HOWARD COBLE, North Carolina
LAMAR SMITH, Texas
STEVEN SCHIFF, New Mexico
ELTON GALLEGLY, California
CHARLES T. CANADY, Florida
BOB INGLIS, South Carolina
BOB GOODLATTE, Virginia
STEPHEN E. BUYER, Indiana
MARTIN R. HOKE, Ohio
SONNY BONO, California
FRED HEINEMAN, North Carolina
ED BRYANT, Tennessee
STEVE CHABOT, Ohio
MICHAEL PATRICK FLANAGAN, Illinois
BOB BARR, Georgia

JOHN CONYERS, JR., Michigan
PATRICIA SCHROEDER, Colorado
BARNEY FRANK, Massachusetts
CHARLES E. SCHUMER, New York
HOWARD L. BERMAN, California
RICK BOUCHER, Virginia
JOHN BRYANT, Texas
JACK REED, Rhode Island
JERROLD NADLER, New York
ROBERT C. SCOTT, Virginia
MELVIN L. WATT, North Carolina
XAVIER BECERRA, California
JOSÉ E. SERRANO, New York
ZOE LOFGREN, California
SHEILA JACKSON LEE, Texas

ALAN F. COFFEY, JR., *General Counsel/Staff Director*
JULIAN EPSTEIN, *Minority Staff Director*

SUBCOMMITTEE ON COURTS AND INTELLECTUAL PROPERTY

CARLOS J. MOORHEAD, California, *Chairman*

F. JAMES SENSENBRENNER, JR., Wisconsin
HOWARD COBLE, North Carolina
BOB GOODLATTE, Virginia
SONNY BONO, California
GEORGE W. GEKAS, Pennsylvania
ELTON GALLEGLY, California
CHARLES T. CANADY, Florida
MARTIN R. HOKE, Ohio

PATRICIA SCHROEDER, Colorado
JOHN CONYERS, JR., Michigan
HOWARD L. BERMAN, California
XAVIER BECERRA, California
RICK BOUCHER, Virginia
JERROLD NADLER, New York

THOMAS E. MOONEY, *Chief Counsel*
JOSEPH V. WOLFE, *Counsel*
MITCH GLAZIER, *Assistant Counsel*
JON DUDAS, *Assistant Counsel*
BETTY WHEELER, *Minority Counsel*

CONTENTS

HEARING DATE

COPYRIGHT ACT TECHNICAL CORRECTIONS

THURSDAY, NOVEMBER 9, 1995

HOUSE OF REPRESENTATIVES,
SUBCOMMITTEE ON COURTS AND
INTELLECTUAL PROPERTY,
COMMITTEE ON THE JUDICIARY,
Washington, DC.

The subcommittee met, pursuant to notice, at 10:13 a.m., in room 2141, Rayburn House Office Building, Hon. Carlos J. Moorhead (chairman of the subcommittee) presiding.

Present: Representatives Carlos J. Moorhead, Howard Coble, Bob Goodlatte, George W. Gekas, Charles T. Canady, and Patricia Schroeder.

Also present: Thomas E. Mooney, chief counsel; Mitch Glazier assistant counsel, Jon Dudas, assistant counsel; Sheila Wood, secretary; and Betty Wheeler, minority counsel.

OPENING STATEMENT OF CHAIRMAN MOORHEAD

Mr. MOORHEAD. The Subcommittee on Courts and Intellectual Property will come to order.

Today the subcommittee is conducting a hearing on H.R. 1861 to make technical corrections in the Satellite Home Viewer Act of 1994 and other provisions of title 17, United States Code. These changes have been suggested by the Copyright Office to make the administration of our copyright laws more clear and easier to administer.

I want to take a moment to compliment the Register of Copyrights, Marybeth Peters, and the Copyright Office. I've worked with the Copyright Office very closely for many years as a member of this subcommittee, and now as chairman. They have always contributed to the work of the Congress in a positive and resourceful way. Many inquiries have been answered and many projects completed on very short notice.

Back when Representative Kastenmeier was the chairman of the subcommittee, I fought hard to make sure that the Copyright Office received the budget it deserves to carry out its important work. I tried to ensure that more positions be created to assist the Register in her duties. I've also communicated to the Librarian of Congress many times the importance of filling positions granted by the Congress and the importance of the Copyright Office.

I remain concerned about the Office and I'm looking forward to learning about the state of the Office today. It is certain that the Copyright Office cannot function optimally without clear, statutory guidance, and that is why we are here today.

There have been several drafting errors in portions of the copyright law and there are other sections which are less clear than they should be. I'm sure my colleagues will agree with me that these technical changes are necessary and timely.

[The bill, H.R. 1861, follows:]

104TH CONGRESS
1ST SESSION

H. R. 1861

To make technical corrections in the Satellite Home Viewer Act of 1994 and other provisions of title 17, United States Code.

IN THE HOUSE OF REPRESENTATIVES

JUNE 15, 1995

Mr. MOORHEAD introduced the following bill; which was referred to the Committee on the Judiciary

A BILL

To make technical corrections in the Satellite Home Viewer Act of 1994 and other provisions of title 17, United States Code.

1   *Be it enacted by the Senate and House of Representa-*

2 *tives of the United States of America in Congress assembled,*

3 **SECTION 1. SATELLITE HOME VIEWER ACT.**

4   The Satellite Home Viewer Act of 1994 (Public Law

5 103–369) is amended as follows:

6   (1) Section 2(3)(A) is amended to read as fol-

7   lows:

8   "(A) in clause (i) by striking '12 cents'

9   and inserting '17.5 cents per subscriber in the

10   case of superstations that as retransmitted by

2

the satellite carrier include any program which,
if delivered by any cable system in the United
States, would be subject to the syndicated exclusivity rules of the Federal Communications
Commission, and 14 cents per subscriber in the
case of superstations that are syndex-proof as
defined in section 258.2 of title 37, Code of
Federal Regulations; and ".

(2) Section 2(4) is amended to read as follows:

"(4) Subsection (c) is amended—

"(A) in paragraph (1)—

"(i) by striking 'until December 31,
1992,';

"(ii) by striking '(2), (3) or (4)' and
inserting '(2) or (3)'; and

"(iii) by striking the second sentence;

"(B) in paragraph (2)—

"(i) in subparagraph (A) by striking
'July 1, 1991' and inserting 'July 1,
1996'; and

"(ii) in subparagraph (D) by striking
'December 31, 1994' and inserting 'December 31, 1999, or in accordance with
the terms of the agreement, whichever is
later'; and

"(C) in paragraph (3)—

"(i) in subparagraph (A) by striking 'December 31, 1991' and inserting 'January 1, 1997';

"(ii) by amending subparagraph (B) to read as follows:

'(B) ESTABLISHMENT OF ROYALTY FEES.—In determining royalty fees under this paragraph, the copyright arbitration royalty panel appointed under chapter 8 shall establish fees for the retransmission of network stations and superstations that most clearly represent the fair market value of secondary transmissions. In determining the fair market value, the panel shall base its decision on economic, competitive, and programming information presented by the parties, including—

'(i) the competitive environment in which such programming is distributed, the cost of similar signals in similar private and compulsory license marketplaces, and any special features and conditions of the retransmission marketplace;

4

'(ii) the economic impact of such fees
2 on copyright owners and satellite carriers;
3 and

4 '(iii) the impact on the continued
5 availability of secondary transmissions to
6 the public.'; and

7 "(iii) in subparagraph (C), by insert-
8 ing 'or July 1, 1997, whichever is later'
9 after 'section 802(g)'.".

10 (3) Section 2(5)(A) is amended to read as fol-
11 lows:

12 "(A) in paragraph (5)(C) by striking 'the
13 date of the enactment of the Satellite Home
14 Viewer Act of 1988' and inserting 'November
15 16, 1988'.".

16 **SEC. 2. DUPLICATIVE PUBLICATION IN FEDERAL REG-**
17 **ISTER.**

18 Section 104A(e)(1)(B)(ii) of title 17, United States
19 Code, is amended by striking the last sentence.

20 **SEC. 3. NEGOTIATED LICENSE FOR JUKEBOXES.**

21 Section 116 of title 17, United States Code, is
22 amended—

23 (1) by amending subsection (b)(2) to read as
24 follows:

5

"(2) ARBITRATION.—Parties not subject to
2 such a negotiation may determine the result of the
3 negotiation by arbitration in accordance with the
4 provisions of chapter 8."; and

5 (2) by adding at the end the following new sub-
6 section:

7 "(d) DEFINITIONS.—As used in this section, the fol-
8 lowing terms mean the following:

9 "(1) A 'coin-operated phonorecord player' is a
10 machine or device that—

11 "(A) is employed solely for the perform-
12 ance of nondramatic musical works by means of
13 phonorecords upon being activated by the inser-
14 tion of coins, currency, tokens, or other mone-
15 tary units or their equivalent;

16 "(B) is located in an establishment making
17 no direct or indirect charge for admission;

18 "(C) is accompanied by a list which is
19 comprised of the titles of all the musical works
20 available for performance on it, and is affixed
21 to the phonorecord player or posted in the e -
22 tablishment in a prominent position where it
23 can be readily examined by the public; and

24 "(D) affords a choice of works available
25 for performance and permits the choice to be

made by the patrons of the establishment in
2 which it is located.

3 "(2) An 'operator' is any person who, alone or
4 jointly with others—

5 "(A) owns a coin-operated phonorecord
6 player;

7 "(B) has the power to make a coin-oper-
8 ated phonorecord player available for placement
9 in an establishment for purposes of public per-
10 formance; or

11 "(C) has the power to exercise primary
12 control over the selection of the musical works
13 made available for public performance on a
14 coin-operated phonorecord player.".

15 **SEC. 4. PUBLIC BROADCASTING COMPULSORY LICENSE.**

16 Section 118 of title 17, United States Code, is
17 amended as follows:

18 (1) Subsection (b) is amended by striking para-
19 graph (1) and redesignating paragraphs (2) and (3)
20 as paragraphs (1) and (2), respectively.

21 (2) Subsection (b)(2) (as redesignated by para-
22 graph (1) of this section) is amended by striking
23 "(2)" each place it appears and inserting "(1)".

24 (3) Subsection (e) is amended to read as fol-
25 lows:

7

"(e)(1) Except as expressly provided in this sub-
2 section, this section shall not apply to works other than
3 those specified in subsection (b).

4 "(2) Owners of copyright in nondramatic literary
5 works and public broadcasting entities may, during the
6 course of voluntary negotiations, agree among themselves,
7 respectively, as to the terms and rates of royalty payments
8 without liability under the antitrust laws. Any such terms
9 and rates of royalty payments shall be effective upon being
10 filed in the Copyright Office, in accordance with regula-
11 tions that the Register of Copyrights shall prescribe.".

12 SEC. 5. REGISTRATION AND INFRINGEMENT ACTIONS.

13 Section 411(b)(1) of title 17, United States Code, is
14 amended to read as follows:

15 "(1) serves notice upon the infringer, not less
16 than 48 hours before such fixation, identifying the
17 work and the specific time and source of its first
18 transmission, and declaring an intention to secure
19 copyright in the work; and".

20 SEC. 6. COPYRIGHT OFFICE FEES.

21 Section 708(b) of title 17, United States Code, is
22 amended to read as follows:

23 "(b)(1) Subject to paragraph (2), in calender year
24 1996 and in any subsequent calendar year, the Register
25 of Copyrights, by regulation, may increase the fees speci-

8

1 fied in subsection (a) by the percent change in the
2 Consumer Price Index published by the Bureau of Labor
3 Statistics, calculated from the month before the last fee
4 became effective to the month before the new fee is pub-
5 lished, rounded off to the nearest dollar, or for a fee less
6 than $12, rounded off to the nearest 50 cents. In the case
7 of a change calculated from 1990, the Consumer Price
8 Index for the month of June 1990 shall be used.

9   "(2) The Register may not increase fees under para-
10 graph (1) at intervals of less than 5 years.".

11 **SEC. 7. COPYRIGHT ARBITRATION ROYALTY PANELS.**

12   (a) ESTABLISHMENT AND PURPOSE.—Section 801 of
13 title 17, United States Code, is amended—

14   (1) in subsection (b)(1) by striking "and 116"
15   in the first sentence and inserting ", 116, and 119";

16   (2) in subsection (c) by inserting after "panel"
17   at the end of the sentence the following:

18 ", including—

19   "(1) authorizing the distribution of those roy-
20   alty fees collected under sections 111, 119, and
21   1005 that the Librarian has found are not subject
22   to controversy; and

23   "(2) accepting or rejecting royalty claims filed
24   under sections 111, 119, and 1007 on the basis of

9

- timeliness or the failure to establish the basis for a
2 claim"; and

3   (3) by amending subsection (d) to read as fol-
4   lows:

5 "(d) SUPPORT AND REIMBURSEMENT OF ARBITRA-
6 TION PANELS.—The Librarian of Congress, upon the rec-
7 ommendation of the Register of Copyrights, shall provide
8 the copyright arbitration royalty panels with the necessary
9 administrative services related to proceedings under this
10 chapter, and shall reimburse the arbitrators at such inter-
11 vals and in such manner as the Librarian shall provide
12 by regulation. Each such arbitrator is an independent con-
13 tractor acting on behalf of the United States, and shall
14 be paid pursuant to a signed agreement between the Li-
15 brary of Congress and the arbitrator. Subject to the provi-
16 sions of section 802(c), payments to the arbitrators shall
17 be considered costs incurred by the Library of Congress
18 and the Copyright Office for purposes of section
19 802(h)(1).".

20   (b) PROCEEDINGS.—Section 802(h)(1) of title 17,
21 United States Code, is amended—

22   (1) by amending the heading to read "DEDUC-
23   TION OF COSTS OF LIBRARY OF CONGRESS AND
24   COPYRIGHT OFFICE FROM ROYALTY FEES.—"; and

10

(2) by inserting before the period at the end of
2 the third sentence the following: ", by assessing 50
3 percent of the costs to the parties who would receive
4 royalties from the royalty rate adopted in the pro-
5 ceeding and 50 percent of the costs to the parties
6 who would pay the royalty rate so adopted".

7 **SEC. 8. DIGITAL AUDIO RECORDING DEVICES AND MEDIA.**

8 Section 1007(b) of title 17, United States Code, is
9 amended by striking "Within 30 days after" in the first
10 sentence and inserting "After".

11 **SEC. 9. EFFECTIVE DATES.**

12 (a) IN GENERAL.—Except as provided in subsection
13 (b), the amendments made by this Act shall take effect
14 on the date of the enactment of this Act.

15 (b) SATELLITE HOME VIEWER ACT.—The amend-
16 ments made by section 1 shall be effective as if enacted
17 as part of the Satellite Home Viewer Act of 1994 (Public
18 Law 103–369).

O

12

Mr. MOORHEAD. Do you have a statement, Mr. Canady?

Mr. CANADY. No statement.

Mr. MOORHEAD. We'll get started very rapidly then. No more opening statements.

Our witness, this morning, will be Ms. Marybeth Peters, who is the Register of Copyrights for the United States. From 1983 to 1994, Ms. Peters held the position of Policy Planning Advisor to the Register. She has also served as Acting General Counsel to the Copyright Office as Chief of both Examining and Information and Reference Division. Ms. Peters holds an undergraduate degree from Rhode Island College and a law degree from the George Washington University. She has served as the consultant on copyright law and the World Intellectual Property Organization and authored the general guide to the Copyright Act of 1976.

Welcome, Ms. Peters. We have your written statement and I ask unanimous consent that it be made a part of the record.

STATEMENT OF MARYBETH PETERS, REGISTER OF COPYRIGHTS, AND ASSOCIATE LIBRARIAN FOR COPYRIGHT SERVICES, U.S. COPYRIGHT OFFICE, LIBRARY OF CONGRESS, ACCOMPANIED BY WILLIAM ROBERTS, SENIOR ATTORNEY FOR COMPULSORY LICENSES, AND MARILYN KRETSINGER, ACTING GENERAL COUNSEL

Ms. PETERS. Thank you very much for the kind words you said about the Copyright Office. I really appreciate them; you have been a flag bearer for the Office and, without you, we wouldn't have been able to do the things that we've been able to do. And, in that regard, I really want to thank you for introducing this bill which really is a technical amendments bill, that will make our life a lot easier and will clarify a number of things. I also thank you for holding this hearing today.

I have brought with me a few of my colleagues. To my right, is Marilyn Kretsinger, the Acting General Counsel, and on my left, Bill Roberts, the Senior Attorney for Compulsory Licenses in the General Counsel's Office, who specializes in licensing issues and on copyright arbitration royalty panel issues.

This technical corrections and clarifications bill would amend the Satellite Home Viewer Act of 1994 and the copyright law in general. We believe that it would permit a more efficient administration of congressionally mandated responsibilities. I think that H.R. 1861 that you have introduced is important legislation, not only for the Copyright Office, but also for the owners and users of the copyright process.

As you noted, I already have a written statement that discusses and analyzes the provisions of the bill, and what I would like to do today is briefly mention some of the highlights of that statement.

The first section of the bill makes technical corrections to the Satellite Home Viewer Act of 1994. Those corrections will make it compatible with the current Copyright Act.

The Satellite Home Viewer Act has not been able to be codified in title 17. As you know, Mr. Chairman, the Copyright Office publishes the copyright law from time to time for the benefit of the public. It is currently called the Green Book. We were not able to integrate the provisions of last year's Satellite Home Viewer Act into our current publication due to drafting errors in the Satellite Home Viewer Act; we have placed it at the back of the book. What we would like to do is issue a publication that fully integrates that law, and the passage of the technical corrections bill would basically make that possible.

Secondly, we would also believe that the section 2 could save us a lot of money. Section 2 of the bill, we believe, is unnecessary, duplicative, and costly. What it would require is publication in the Federal Register of annual, cumulative listings of works in which notices of intent to enforce restored copyrights have been filed.

By law we are obliged to publish these notices in the Federal Register every 4 months. We will have a cumulative list available in our Public Information Office and in our search rooms. Additionally, information on all notices of intent to enforce a restored copyright will be fully catalogued and will be available online both at the Library of Congress, through Internet and through various online service providers. Those who will be affected by this have all agreed that it would be so costly to publish this huge list in the Federal Register. So we believe that this provision serves no purpose and simply would entail a great expense.

Sections 3 and 4 of the bill clarify application of the copyright arbitration royalty panel process to certain proceedings under the jukebox license and the public broadcasting compulsory license. These sections correct an oversight in the Copyright Royalty Tribunal Reform Act of 1993 which did not refer to these proceedings.

Section 6 of the bill clarifies what I believe was Congress' intent in 1990, when it changed the law to allow the Copyright Office to increase its fees in accordance with the Consumer Price Index. The present law allows the Copyright Office to increase the fees in 1995 and in each subsequent 5-year period. In 1995, the Copyright Office did not raise the fees because the rise in the Consumer Price Index was only about 16 percent. That would allow us to raise the registration fee from $20 to $23.30.

A Copyright Office task force on fee services found that the revenue realized by this increase would be less than $.5 million and concluded that our administrative costs in raising the fees would result in a net loss to the Copyright Office and that, coupled with the operation disruption, that would last for many years because of the fee increase, led to the conclusion that the fee should not be raised in 1995.

The problem is that the current law states that the fees cannot be raised until the year 2000, and we believe the law provides that the increase in the year 2000 would have to be based on the increase in the Consumer Price Index from 1995 to the year 2000, not 1990 to the year 2000. We believe it would be preferable to allow the Copyright Office to raise fees in any year and cumulate the Consumer Price Index from the last fee increase. We also agree that fees should not be raised more than once every 5 years.

Section 7 resolves a serious fee problem with respect to arbitrators selected to serve on a copyright arbitration royalty panel. As the system stands now, the Library of Congress contracts with the arbitrators to serve on a panel, but it's without authority to pay them. Instead, the arbitrators must make arrangement for payment directly with the litigants before them. Your bill avoids confusion and disputes among litigants over the means of payment to the arbitrators, and it would allow the Copyright Office to pay arbitrators directly from corresponding royalty funds.

In sum, Mr. Chairman, this bill provides the copyright law and the administrative process with the clarity and efficiency that it needs, and I thank you for giving me the opportunity to appear before you and to answer any questions that you may have.

[The prepared statement of Ms. Peters follows:]

PREPARED STATEMENT OF MARYBETH PETERS, REGISTER OF COPYRIGHTS AND ASSOCIATE LIBRARIAN FOR COPYRIGHT SERVICES, U.S. COPYRIGHT OFFICE, LIBRARY OF CONGRESS

Thank you for the opportunity to testify on H.R. 1861 which Chairman Moorhead introduced on June 15, 1995. This bill would make technical corrections to the Satellite Home Viewer Act of 1994 and other provisions of title 17. These amendments are technical corrections or clarifications that would permit more efficient administration of congressionally mandated responsibilities. My statement briefly summarize each of the technical corrections or other clarifications included in the bill.

I. SUMMARY AND COMMENT ON SECTIONS OF H.R. 1861

A. Section 1. "Satellite Home Viewer Act"

Section 1 of the proposed bill makes corrections to the Satellite Home Viewer Act, later sections make corrections to title 17. The Satellite Home Viewer Act of 1994 (Pub.L. No. 103–369) contained several drafting errors which need immediate correction in order for the Act to be codified properly in title 17. Some but not all of the errors were recognized in H.R. 5303, a bill introduced for the record by Chairman Hughes on November 29, 1994. The errors were the result of the amendments to the Copyright Act enacted in 1994 which did not take into account the changes made in the law by the Copyright Royalty Tribunal Reform Act of 1993.

Subsection (1) clarifies the royalty rates that are to be paid by satellite carriers for carriage of network and superstation signals. The Satellite Home Viewer Act of 1994 appears to have inadvertently reversed the royalty rates for superstations, requiring satellite carriers to pay 17.5 cents for signals not subject to the FCC's syndicated exclusivity rules, and 14 cents per subscriber for signals subject to such rules. The intended result, adopting the 1992 arbitration panel decision under the Satellite Home Viewer Act of 1988, is the other way around. 1991 Satellite Carrier Rate Adjustment, 57 FR 19052 (May 1, 1992). H.R. 1861 clarifies the application of the rates by using the term "syndex-proof" to indicate those signals not subject to the FCC syndicated exclusivity rules. This term was used by the arbitration panel, adopted by the Copyright Royalty Tribunal in its rules, and is now defined in the Copyright Office rules. 37 C.F.R. 258.2.

Subsection (2) makes technical changes to the Satellite Home Viewer Act. It corrects the section numbers, and accompanying references, to recognize the changes made to title 17 in 1993 by the Copyright Royalty Tribunal Reform Act. The criteria to be used by the 1997 arbitration panel to fashion new royalty rates are repeated verbatim to show that they properly amend § 119(c)(3)(B) rather than incorrectly replace § 119(c)(3)(D), which would have eliminated the provision identifying which persons are subject to paying § 119 royalty fees.

Subsection (3) simply deletes reference to the effective date of the Satellite Home Viewer Act of 1988 to avoid the confusion resulting from two Acts of the same name, and inserts the effective date of the Satellite Home Viewer Act of 1988, which was November 16, 1988.

B. Section 2, "Duplicative Publication in Federal Register"

Section 2 of H.R. 1861 deletes the second sentence of section 104A(e)(1)(B)(ii) set out in section 514(a) of Public Law 103–65 which requires the Copyright Office to publish in the Federal Register a cumulative list of notices of intent to enforce restored copyrights filed with the Office. The Office is already required to publish a list of such notices in the Federal Register every four months. Interested parties have already indicated that an annual publication would be expensive and would serve no purpose; moreover, the Copyright Office will have a cumulative and more detailed record available online in the Office and through the Internet.

C. Section 3, "Negotiated Licenses for Jukeboxes"

Section 3 of H.R. 1861 makes two changes to the § 116 jukebox license. The Copyright Royalty Tribunal Reform Act eliminated the old § 116 jukebox compulsory license and replaced it with the 116A negotiated jukebox license adopted during implementation of the Berne Convention in 1989. The replacement has produced two unintended results: elimination of the definitions of a jukebox and a jukebox operator, and creation of an arbitration proceeding which is arguably not a copyright arbitration royalty panel (CARP) proceeding. The bill restores the original definitional provisions and clarifies that all jukebox negotiated licenses which require arbitration are CARP proceedings.

D. Section 4, "Public Broadcasting Compulsory License"

Section 4 of H.R. 1861 eliminates an inconsistency caused by the 1993 Copyright Royalty Tribunal Reform Act in the § 118 public broadcasting compulsory license. This Act directed the Librarian of Congress to collect royalty rate proposals from public broadcasters and copyright owners and then to "proceed" on the basis of the proposals." Formerly, the Copyright Royalty Tribunal would receive such proposals and then conduct a proceeding. The 1993 Act struck each reference to the Tribunal in 118 and inserted the Librarian of Congress each place it appeared. Ratemaking authority for § 118, however, lies exclusively with the CARPS; therefore, the Librarian cannot "proceed" with the rate proposals. H.R. 1861 therefore eliminates the procedure of having the parties submit their proposals to the Librarian.

H.R. 1861 also eliminates subsection (e)(2) of § 118, which required the Copyright Office to submit a report to Congress in 1980 as to the extent of voluntarily negotiated public broadcasting licenses.

E. Section 5, "Registration and Infringement Actions"

Section 5 changes the period of advance notice that copyright owners must give to infringers of their intent to secure copyright in the fixation of a live performance from not less than 10 days to not less than 48 hours. This provision has traditionally applied primarily to the broadcasting of sporting events. Copyright owners of sporting events have had great difficulty in giving infringers 10 days notice because often the teams and the time of the game are not known 10 days in advance. For example, in any league in which teams are eliminated by playoffs, who the teams are that will reach the final round, where they will play, and at what time, cannot be known until the semifinals have finished. This amendment is sought by sports owners and will alleviate this very real problem.

F. Section 6, "Copyright Office Fees"

Section 6 adds a necessary clarification to 17 USC 708(b). In 1990 Congress added a new subsection (B) to section 708 authorizing the Copyright Office to raise its fees in 1995 and in each subsequent fifth calendar year to reflect increases in the Consumer Price Index (CPI). Whenever the Copyright Office considers whether to raise fees, it must also examine the costs for the Office associated with such an increase. In 1994 when the Office considered whether it should increase fees in 1995 based on the CPI, it concluded that the costs to the Office of raising the fee would be more than the amount it could recapture by the increased fee. The Office, therefore, decided that although it had the authority to do so, it would not increase fees in 1995. In examining section 708(b), the Office could not, however, determine whether it would have to wait until the year 2000 to raise fees, or whether it could do so in 1996, and whether, when it made an increase it could use 1990 as the beginning date from which the fee basis was determined, or if it would be limited to the changes since 1995. The proposed legislation would clarify Congress' intent in the 1990 legislation by giving the Office the authority to increase fees based on the CPI at any calendar year but no more frequently than at five year intervals and to make the fee adjustment based on the CPI increase from the last fee adjustment.

G. Section 7, "Copyright Arbitration Royalty Panels"

Section 7 clarifies several important administrative issues regarding the operation of the Copyright Arbitration Royalty Panels (CARPs). First, and most importantly, the Librarian of Congress would be given express authority to pay the CARP arbitrators directly both in ratemaking and distribution proceedings. This is achieved by clarifying that the deduction of the Library's and Copyright Office's costs already provided for in the statute at 17 U.S.C. 802(h)(1) includes the arbitrators' costs. Allowing the Library to pay the arbitrators avoids confusion and disputes among the parties over the means of payment and eliminates ad hoc payment schemes. The bill also clarifies that in a ratemaking proceeding, copyright owners and users are responsible for the Library of Congress and the Copyright Office's costs in equal shares. The first CARP panel begins next week and both arbitrators and parties are concerned about how payment is to be made.

Two other aspects of the Copyright Office's authority to administer CARP proceedings are also clarified by H.R. 1861: its ability to distribute royalties not in controversy, and its authority to reject royalty claims on the basis of timeliness or the failure to state a claim.

Finally, the bill also clarifies that the 1997 ratemaking proceeding for the § 119 satellite carrier compulsory license and all satellite carrier royalty distribution proceedings are CARP proceedings.

H. Section 8, "Digital Audio Recording Devices and Media"

Section 8 makes a change necessary for administrative efficiency. The Audio Home Recording Act requires DART royalty distribution proceedings to begin 30 days after the last date for the filing of claims; namely, March 30 of each year. However, because of the provisions that claims are valid if they are mailed with the U.S. Postal Service by the last day of February, many valid claims are still being accepted in early March. The requirement to begin a proceeding on March 30 is not only burdensome on the participating parties—who must negotiate settlements and put together a case against those who do not settle with less than a month's notice of who the claimants are—but conflicts with the Copyright Office's precontroversy discovery procedure. The Copyright Office's has already been required to miss the 30-day starting requirement on two occasions due to sheer necessity and with the full agreement of the parties, and annual missing of the starting date is inevitable. The bill remedies the situation by directing the Librarian to convene a CARP anytime after 30 days after the last date for the filing of claims.

I. Section 9, "Effective dates"

Section 9 establishes the effective dates. All amendments made to the Copyright Act by H.R. 1861 take effect on the date of enactment of the legislation, with the exception of the § 119 satellite carrier provisions, which because they are only correcting drafting errors, are effective on the date of the Satellite Home Viewer Act of 1994 was enacted (October 18, 1994).

II. CONCLUSION

This bill will eliminate inadvertent errors that threaten to hinder the Copyright Office's effective execution of its duties. The Copyright Office fully supports this legislation.

Mr. MOORHEAD. Thank you. I'll recognize the gentleman from North Carolina.

Mr. COBLE. Ms. Peters, how are you?

Ms. PETERS. I'm just fine, thank you.

Mr. COBLE. Good to have you all here. Mr. Chairman, my question does not relate to the issue at hand, but while we have the luxury of your presence, Ms. Peters, I want to run this by you, because an inquiry was put to me yesterday.

A recent decision in the ninth circuit, the La Cienega—am I pronouncing that correctly——

Ms. PETERS. La Cienega.

Mr. COBLE [continuing]. Has cast a cloud of doubt over the copyright status of a large number of musical works created prior to January 1, 1978. Now, as I understand it, Ms. Peters, the ninth circuit case is in direct conflict with a longstanding second circuit case (a); (b) the Supreme Court has denied cert; (c) it appears to me that legislation may be the next appropriate remedy. Now, am I on course so far?

Ms. PETERS. A hundred percent.

Mr. COBLE. OK, good. And, as I have been told, Ms. Peters, and, Mr. Chairman, you may know about this as well, I think the issue involves a work or song that had been recorded and released, and the issue, I presume, is whether or not this constitutes publication and/or registration? And, since you say I'm on course 100 percent, do you agree with me that legislation is probably desirable?

Ms. PETERS. Yes. Actually, I've been working on this myself because it really directly affects the day-to-day practices of the Copyright Office, because we still register works that were created before 1978. We have day-to-day practices that are exactly at odds with the ninth circuit, and I had hoped that the Supreme Court would take the case and basically resolve the issue, but it hasn't.

There's a very old copyright case that involved piano rolls; it said that a piano roll was not a copy of the musical composition embodied on it. It was merely a mechanical reproduction, not a copy. Only copies publish copyright works before 1978. Therefore, distribution of recordings would not, under our practices, and we believe under the 1909 act, publish a musical composition. Therefore, if anyone sent the Office a recording with an application and fee for registration of a song as a published work, we would write back saying that recording is not a copy, therefore, the music had not been published. If the recording happened to have a copyright notice, which most of the time it would not, we would still not register the recording as a published musical composition. We would suggest that, unless sheet music—an eye readable copy that could be read at—unless sheet music copies had been offered for sale or made generally available, the work was not published. We would then register the song as an unpublished work. Twenty-eight years later, on the basis of the unpublished registration, the composer would renew the copyright for a second term. If sheet music copies were published, we would register the musical composition as published, and the renewal would be based on that.

What this case does is say, if a recording was released before 1978 and if that recording did not contain the proper copyright notice, and I can tell you that probably 99.9 percent did not, that musical composition went into the public domain. This holding will affect most songs created before 1978; even serious classical music compositions as well as the more popular songs were recorded and these recordings were distributed to the public.

So, I think what you have is much of the pre-1978 musical compositions under a cloud under the ninth circuit decision, and it affects what we do now day-in and day-out. People won't know whether to pay royalties or not, they won't know the value of their catalog. It seems incongruous that at the time that this subcommittee is considering lengthening the copyright term, in part, to give musical compositions that were created before 1978 a longer term, those compositions may have no copyright at all.

Mr. COBLE. Well, I thank you for that, Ms. Peters. And, Mr. Chairman, I'm thinking aloud now, idle hours are at a premium around here. We don't have too many idle hours these days, but I'm thinking, Mr. Chairman, in the form of a suggestion; it might be a good idea for our subcommittee to maybe have a prayer meeting with the Copyright Office at an appropriate time.

Ms. PETERS. Within a day or so I will be sending you some possible legislative language. The problem is that, what you're trying to clarify is a law that is no longer in existence. The question is, can you pass a bill that is a finding or declaration that publication of music under the 1909 act did not include distribution of recordings of musical compositions? I think there's got to be a way to do this.

Mr. COBLE. Well, I appreciate your response.

And, Mr. Chairman, I thank you for having recognized me.

Mr. MOORHEAD. The gentleman from Virginia.

Mr. GOODLATTE. Thank you, Mr. Chairman. And, welcome, Ms. Peters.

Ms. PETERS. Thank you.

Mr. GOODLATTE. We're glad to have you with us. I understand, from your testimony, that the first Copyright Arbitration Royalty Panel or CARP—I think we need a new acronym there—I understand you'll be in panel next week. How will this legislation help the CARP panels in that specific hearing and in general?

Ms. PETERS. I could try to answer that, but actually, on my left I have my resident expert. And, I'm going to ask Bill to answer that question.

Mr. GOODLATTE. Certainly.

Mr. ROBERTS. Good morning.

We have right now, of course, as you indicated, the start of a CARP proceeding to distribute royalties collected under the cable compulsory license for the years 1990, 1991, and 1992. The distribution will be about $500 million, and we have already selected the three arbitrators to serve on that panel.

A serious problem that we have is with the billing for the arbitrators. We do not currently have authority to deduct the cost of the arbitrators from the royalty fees, so we have a complication with now the arbitrators are uncertain as to how and under what means they will be compensated. We know at what rate they have specified, how many dollars per hour they will charge, but they have to work out with the parties an arrangement for payment and the terms of that payment, and it's going to be an added burden on the parties as well as the arbitrators and a time-consuming effort distracting from the proceeding while they work out the means and method of payment.

The proposal and the bill would simply allow us—we already are allowed to deduct our cost, the cost of the Copyright Office from the royalty fee—the bill will allow us to, in addition to our cost, to deduct the cost of the arbitrators right off the top of the royalty pool and make payment directly to them under terms that we can come to agreement with the arbitrators. So it's a much more efficient system and it eliminates the problem of the parties having to work out an arrangement with the arbitrators once the proceeding is started.

Ms. PETERS. Let me add one more thing. It would also clarify the issue with regard to what proceedings are subject to the CARPS, which was, I think, an oversight. It would also clear up certain precontroversy procedures such as the decision to distribute royalties not in controversy. It would also give us clear authority to dismiss late or insufficient claims, and it would also direct all proposals for public broadcasting rates to go to a CARP and not to the Librarian of Congress, who has no authority to deal with them.

Mr. GOODLATTE. Thank you. What problems do you have in raising fees and why did you decide not to raise fees in 1995?

Ms. PETERS. I tried to anticipate that in my statement. The problem that we had is we can only take into account the Consumer Price Index increases and that that was about 16 percent, which brought us to $23.30, which is not a great number for applicants, and that we would only basically get about a half a million dollars.

When we change fees—we register more than 700,000 works each year from all over the world—every publication, every form has to be changed to reflect that fee. It takes years for people to figure out what the right fee is and so we have the cost of changing the publications, but for many years we have had the problem of most of the material coming in with the wrong fee and then having to write for the right fee. Since we could only raise the fee by about $3 and we would be gaining so little money, we decided there would be a net loss to us, not a net gain. And, even today, the fees were raised in 1991, and even today we get a number of fees that are wrong—that are the old fee, not the 1991 fee. So it was basically a decision that we would come out a net loser rather than a net winner.

Mr. GOODLATTE. So now does the law allow you to accumulate that——

Ms. PETERS. That's the issue. We believe that at the point that we hit maybe $25, it might make sense to raise the fee, but we can't raise it until the year 2000 under the current law, and then it's not clear that we could cumulate from 1990 to the year 2000. So we're basically trying to say that we should be able to raise the fee when it makes sense and cumulate up to that point, but once we do that, we can't do it for another 5 years, not that we would ever do that, given the amount of work that's involved in changing the fee.

Mr. GOODLATTE. So I take it you think that Congress should reconsider tying the fees to the CPI?

Ms. PETERS. No. We basically agree that it can be tied to the CPI; we want you to authorize us to cumulate the rise in the CPI up to a point where it makes sense to change the fee and then say you can't change the fee for 5 more years. We do not want you to specify a specific year and then say only cumulate up to that year. The way I read the statute, since we didn't raise the fee in 1995 we can't consider the past 5 years. You go from 1995 forward, not from 1990 to 2000.

Mr. GOODLATTE. Now what would be your thoughts on simply letting the Office raise the fees as it deems necessary based on a fair finding and determination by your Office with the option of rejection of such an increase by the Congress?

Ms. PETERS. You could do that and we wouldn't object. I was being much more conservative because fees are your——

Mr. GOODLATTE. That you wouldn't object?

Ms. PETERS. No. We wouldn't. No, we wouldn't object. I think that authors might object. In the past, the amount of the fee has been a very political issue with people wanting to make sure that it was kept low, even below cost. And, it's my recollection for the 30 years I've been in the Office there have been a number of groups that have been very vehement about the level of the registration fee.

But, I assume that what you're suggesting—we then would do the work to determine a reasonable and fair fee and you would then review the work; that seems fine.

Mr. GOODLATTE. Well, I think the purpose for doing something like that would be to allow you to meet your requirements in terms of as copyright laws change, as you have new requirements to fulfill to meet your responsibilities in hiring more employees, and so on, in a way that you can better plan than——

Ms. PETERS. No, we would actually like that. I just wasn't bold enough to suggest it.

Mr. GOODLATTE. All right. Well, have you had problems in hiring the employees that you need to carry out your necessary functions?

Ms. PETERS. We have not had problems finding qualified individuals. We've had problems in part because the Library of Congress is under a court order to redo all of its hiring practices, and that is a very, very slow process. So, the average time to bring someone on board is between 8 months and 12 months. And, yes, that's a very serious problem.

Mr. GOODLATTE. But it's not so much related to budgetary constraints as it is to judicial constraints?

Ms. PETERS. That's true. That is correct.

Mr. GOODLATTE. OK. Are there any changes in this Office that are not found in the—any changes that you would recommend for your Office that are not contained in the chairman's bill?

Ms. PETERS. Yes, thank you. We've been looking at what we could do that basically would reflect better fiscal policy and make us able to fulfill our statutory needs even better. And, I have one suggestion, we have prepaid fees in what are called deposit accounts. These are where a publisher will prepay the registration or recordation fee. They will send us for example, $500 and as the registrations come through, we apply that money, but for much of the year the money is inactive—it sits in the Treasury. It's about $2½ million just sitting.

We've been thinking about the possibility of seeking investment authority so that we could earn interest on that money. We figure that we could earn between—you could only prudently invest a part of it—but, even if you invested only 30 or 40 percent, we believe could earn up to $50,000 a year. It would be extremely helpful if we could use that money to build the new Copyright Office electronic registration system. This system will be very, very costly to build. The people who have deposit accounts are the big publishers who would be the biggest beneficiaries of the electronic system.

We would like you to consider this—the ability to invest the deposit account money, the prepaid money, in interest-bearing treasury securities, and then use that interest for the building of the electronic copyright registration, deposit, and recordation system.

Mr. GOODLATTE. Thank you. Thank you, Mr. Chairman.

Mr. MOORHEAD. The gentlelady from Colorado.

Mrs. SCHROEDER. Mr. Chairman, I apologize to the witness and the committee for being a little late this morning.

The only question I have is, does anybody know of any controversy about this bill?

Ms. PETERS. I do not. Do you? No.

Mrs. SCHROEDER. Good. That's all I wanted on the record. Thank you very much, Mr. Chairman.

Ms. PETERS. Hopefully, if people had problems you would hear from them; we have not heard from anyone.

Mr. MOORHEAD. I recognize now our latest hero from Pennsylvania who recently fought off robbers and recovered his car.

Mr. GEKAS. Not hero, dumb cop. But, Mr. Chairman, thank you for recognizing me. In this legislation, I am not up to snuff on each one of the provisions that is sought to be amended by the technical changes. So in a large part, I'm going to rely on the chairman and his staff to guide me through the process. I'm going to repose confidence in them to give us a bill that will accomplish the intended purpose and I will support the chairman in that endeavor. I have nothing further to say.

Mr. MOORHEAD. I have just one question I wanted to ask, and that is, you say that the starting date of DART controversies need to be later than March 30. Do you have an idea of when you expect to start DART controversies this year?

Ms. PETERS. The way that the change is worded, it would be, instead of by March 30, it would be after March 30. Our expectation is that the parties really want to resolve this as quickly as possible and it would take place within a few months. We did not put a date certain because, based on one of the proceedings that's in front of us, they're having a very difficult time trying to settle it.

The amount of money that comes in under this fund is extremely small. If they do not settle, I'm not sure that there's enough money in the fund to pay the parties. So settlement is absolutely critical. But the bottom line is we generally expect resolution within a few months.

Mr. MOORHEAD. I understand you'll send us your recommendations on the pre-1978 situations?

Ms. PETERS. Yes.

Mr. MOORHEAD. Before our break?

Ms. PETERS. Yes. Oh, yes. Within the next day or two you could have it.

Mr. MOORHEAD. We'll look forward to getting it and try to see that it's a bill order and perhaps get it introduced.

Ms. PETERS. Thank you very much.

Mr. MOORHEAD. The meeting is adjourned.

[Whereupon, at 10:43 a.m., the subcommittee adjourned.]

O

CPSIA information can be obtained
at www.ICGtesting.com
Printed in the USA
LVHW052001121218
600215LV00018B/835/P

9 781333 781644